Ukulele Songbook
Heavy Metal Hits For Ukulele

Adrian Gavinson

Adrian Gavinson

Copyright © 2018 Adrian Gavinson

A&M Books

All rights reserved.

Ukulele Songbook: Heavy Metal Hits For Ukulele

SONGBOOK CONTENTS:

1. Introduction to Metal Ukulele **(1)**

- **Tuning Up**
- **Tabs**
- **Chords**

2. Basics of Metal Ukulele **(23)**

- **Technique 1: The Phrygian Scale (Mode)**
- **Technique 2: Playing Riffs**

3. Metal Songs For Ukulele **(35)**

4. Conclusion **(73)**

Ukulele Songbook
Heavy Metal Hits For Ukulele

Introduction to Metal Ukulele

Welcome to the book of metal songs for ukulele. Before we get going with the head-banging and metal music, I'd like to take this opportunity to thank you for choosing this songbook. Ukulele is by far the greatest instrument on the planet and in the case of this songbook, whoever said you can't play metal on the ukulele is a liar and we're about to prove them wrong. Either way, I hope you find this songbook to be useful and I wish you all the best with your ukulele journey both in the context of this book and in the future.

How To Use This Songbook

Primarily, this is a songbook with a diverse range of metal tunes and melodies for you to try out. However, don't be fooled. We aren't just going to provide a bland bunch of tunes without context. The secondary aim of this book is to teach you some elements of metal ukulele so that you can write your own banging metal riffs and licks using the knowledge that you hopefully will acquire from this book. In this way, this book is broken up into two halves: some theory where we will look at what it takes to write and play metal ukulele, and then we will look at some riffs that have been inspired by all time greats. I will finally add that where there is no specified time signature, every tab in this book is in 4/4 with 120 tempo.

Without further ado, let's begin.

What is a ukulele?

One of my favourite questions to ask students when they first start out is - *what is a ukulele*? I ask this question simply to hear their response. The answer to this is often telling as to what they expect out of the instrument and how they perceive it. More often than not, their answers are mistaken and false. So just in case, you don't know much about the ukulele, this chapter is invaluable as a resource for you. It is vital to know what a ukulele is and where it fits in as a stringed instrument.

Let us get one misconception out of the way from the get-go - a ukulele is **not** a guitar and in no way should be treated or seen as one. It isn't even in the guitar family. The ukulele's appearance might lead you to believe this, but the truth is that it's in a family of its own - the ukulele family. In this family, there are ukuleles of all sizes. From smallest to largest, we have : soprano, concert, tenor, baritone and bass. There are other instruments that are hybrids such as the kiku (also known as the guitalele) and the banjolele, the mandolele.

What am I telling you that ukuleles are not guitars? Because a lot of newbies think you can just pick up a ukulele and start strumming it wildly like it's a guitar - don't! Ukuleles are smaller and much more fragile than guitars with nylon strings that break easily when too much pressure is applied.

The Ukulele: A Brief History

The ukulele is a small 4 stringed instrument that originates in the state of Hawaii. It is believed that Portuguese settlers introduced the instrument to the island and since the 20th century, it has gained very wide-spread popularity. The internet age of the 2000s and even more-so, the 2010s has made the ukulele a staple of popular music and it has been used by a huge range of artists across genres. While it is iconically used in folk, country and some forms of pop music, the ukulele has also featured in punk rock, metal and jazz-fusion.

The bottom line? The ukulele is a very sought after instrument and its sound is well liked and quite popular in music right now. Good thing you're here to learn it right?

So now that we've taken a quick look at the history of the instrument, it's time to focus on the ukulele itself and its many parts. Take a look at page 6.

The Ukulele and its Parts

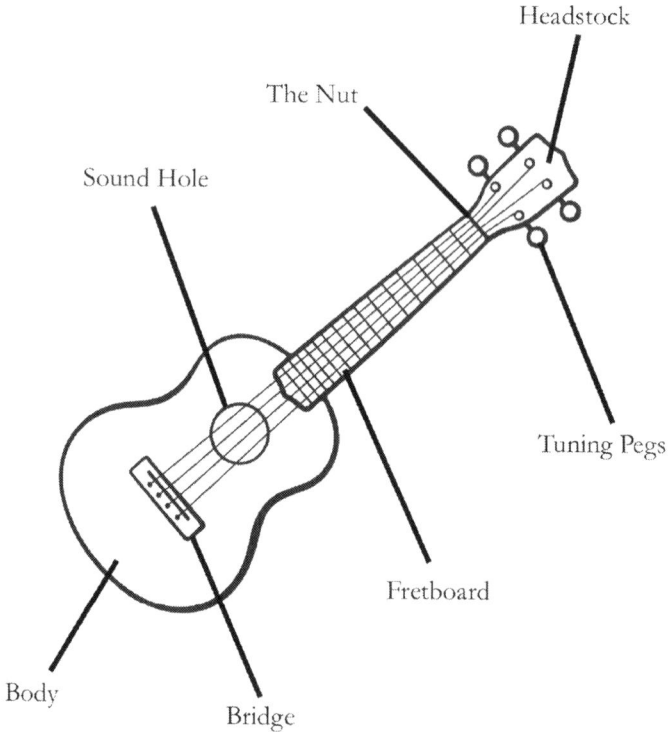

Now that you've had a glance at the various parts of the ukulele, it's time to explain what everything is and what each part is for.

The Headstock

Beginning with the headstock of the ukulele, this fragile part holds the tuners of the ukulele which you turn to tune the instrument. It also links the neck, fretboard and nut - all of which, we'll get to in a moment. In essence, the headstock is a very delicate part of the instrument and any bumps can cause serious damage to the ukulele and its sound. Therefore, treat this part with respect and apart from when you tune the ukulele, avoid touching it at all costs. Never pick up the ukulele from its headstock - always from the neck. Be careful carrying your ukulele around and it would be wise to buy a padded carrier case to avoid unnecessary stress and costs.

Tuning Pegs

Following on from the headstock, it makes sense to talk about the tuning pegs - which are also called tuners. There are 4 tuning pegs, one for each string and they sit adjacent to one another in the headstock of the ukulele. They are also fragile.

Any small movement can severely alter the tuning and pitch of the ukulele. Therefore, when tuning up (in the next chapter), take a great deal of care and move the pegs slowly and not in an erratic or fast motion.

The Nut

While the uses of the headstock and tuning pegs might appear obvious, the purpose of the nut might not be - at first glance. It is a tiny thin white plastic-y bar that sits on the edge of the headstock and conjoins it to the neck. It has four little slits, each for the strings to sit on as they move towards the tuners. **So, what does it do?** Believe it or not, the ukulele nut is one of, if not, the most important element of the tonality and tuning of the instrument. If damaged, you might as well get a new ukulele because the cost of repair is pretty astronomical. It essentially acts as a balancing force which helps the strings retain their elasticity and tension. Make sure you don't start messing with it and ensure it is given respect - just like all the parts of the instrument.

The Sound Hole

Probably the most self-explanatory part of the ukulele - the sound hole is the hole of the instrument which emits the sound. Just like acoustic guitars and other acoustic stringed instruments, the sound created when playing a note or strumming a chord is let out via the sound hole. There isn't too much more to say about it other than the fact that one benefit of playing the ukulele is that you don't need to worry about losing picks inside the hole. Not only is the hole likely too small for you to drop a pick inside of it, but ukulele typically aren't played with picks.

Fretboard

The fretboard is the part of the ukulele that you put your fingers on to play notes. The fretboard is lined with metallic lines which are called 'frets'. They are perfectly and mathematically the right distance apart to create a difference in pitch. As you move up the fretboard, the higher pitch a note is.

The Bridge

The bridge is a wooden piece on the other side of the ukulele to the area we have been focusing on. This joins the strings to the nut and is where the strings are tied up in a small knot. When changing strings, if you've never done it before, it might be wise to go to a local guitar or music store and have a specialist do it for you. This will avoid string and bridge damage.

The Body

Finally, we have the body of the ukulele. This is shaped like a small guitar and helps to round the ukulele's form off quite perfectly. The body is also a delicate part of the instrument and much of the shape is for aesthetic reasons only. Either way, be sure not to bump it around. Damage can be costly. Unlike acoustic guitars, ukulele are smaller so it's harder to rest them on your lap while playing sitting down.

How To Tune Your Ukulele

Well done! You've completed the introduction section of this book and should now be somewhat familiar with the ins and outs of the instrument. We are very close to the playing aspect of the ukulele but before we even play a single note, we have to tune the ukulele. A well tuned ukulele is a great-sounding one.

The ukulele has **four** strings and they are tuned from top (nearest to your chest) to bottom (nearest to your legs) as follows:

G - C - E - A

Whilst you could invest in a cheap tuner which clips onto the headstock of your ukulele, it's much more convenient and time-efficient to just use online tuners which can be downloaded in the form of apps. Alternatively, you can find many 'how to tune your ukulele' videos online too which play the sound of each string and you can match your ukulele's strings to each of the four pitches. In any case, remember to go back and tune your ukulele twice to ensure each string is well tuned with accuracy. There is nothing worse than an even slightly out of tune instrument. No matter how well you can play notes and chords, it will sound very bad if your instrument is off by a few pitches. Trust me when I say that it's worth the extra few seconds or minutes that it takes to be pedantic about your ukulele's tuning.

Now, in case you're wondering which string is which, it is simple - the **G** string is the string closest to your body. It is often called the top string. Next, we have the **C** string which is actually the deepest sounding string. Then this is followed by the **E** string and of course, the bottom string (which is the one closest to your legs) - the **A** string. The ukulele naturally has a distinctively sweet open tuning. In fact, a nice little thing to do once your ukulele is in tune is to let each string ring out - one by one. Become accustomed to the vibrancy of the ukulele and how it melodically resounds.

Reading Tablature

Now that you have a well-tuned instrument, it's time to get down to some playing. Before we actually strum or pick any old note, it's important to understand how ukulele players read music. It ought to be stated here that while numerous professional ukulele players can and do read 'traditional sheet music', it is surprisingly uncommon for a ukulele player or guitarist to use such a form of scored sheet music on a stave.

Instead, ukulele players frequently use **'tablature'**. Tablature is often shortened to 'tabs' and it refers to a score that looks like this:

As you will notice in the diagram above, there are four lines. These lines represent the strings of the ukulele. The bottom line represents the string closest to you (the **G** string), the next one along is the **C**

string, then this is followed by the **E** string and the high string (the nearest one to your legs) is the **A** string.

Now, you might have realised that the four lines have nothing on them. That's because the diagram on the previous page is just a blank tab slate. When you add numbers, you have notes to play. Tablature is a way to show the ukulele player what notes we have to play and when a number is added to a line (string), this represents what fret (line space on the ukulele) we have to play.

Look at the diagram below:

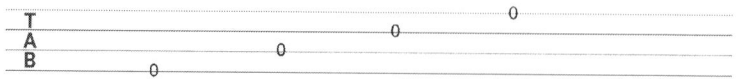

Notice how there is a '**0**' on each string. Since we are not playing a fret, the numbered fret is technically zero. We call this an open string and such are always written as a '**0**' on the tablature slate.

When we do add fretted notes to the tab, it would look something like this:

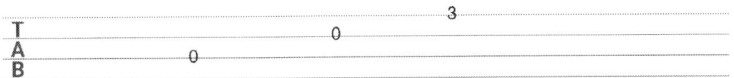

In this example, we have one fretted note and two open string. So, in order to play the melody above, we first play the open second string (the **C** string). After, we play the open **E** string. Finally, we play the third fret (third lined space on the fretboard of the ukulele) of the (top) **A** string.

Melodies are a series of notes which are usually played individually. However, it must be emphasised that there is a difference between **grouped notes** and **individual notes** and how they are distinguished when written out in tablature form. Let us take the example of the diagram above - take a look at the following two variations of the same notes. One is played as individual notes (identical to the diagram above) and one is grouped.

(1)

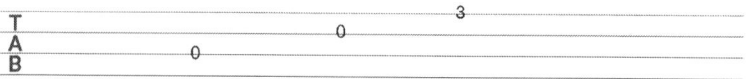

(2)

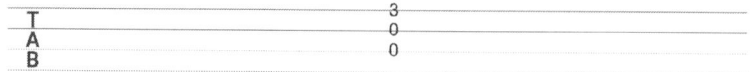

Both variations involve the same notation : that which makes up a **C major chord**. They both have two open strings and end on the third fret of the high **A** string. Nonetheless, there is a very key difference between diagrams (1) and (2). That is that there is a spacing in diagram (1) that is not found in diagram (2). The notes of the first diagram are separated and played individually, whereas the notes in the second one are played together in what we call a chord. A **chord** is a group of two or more notes. In the case of diagram (2), the notes are played in unison. When notes are grouped in a chord, we are actually supposed to strum in one motion.

This allows the strings to ring out and in the case of this example, we hear a gorgeous C major chord - one of the most important beginner's ukulele chords!

Now let's explore chords in more depth. Turn over and we shall continue…

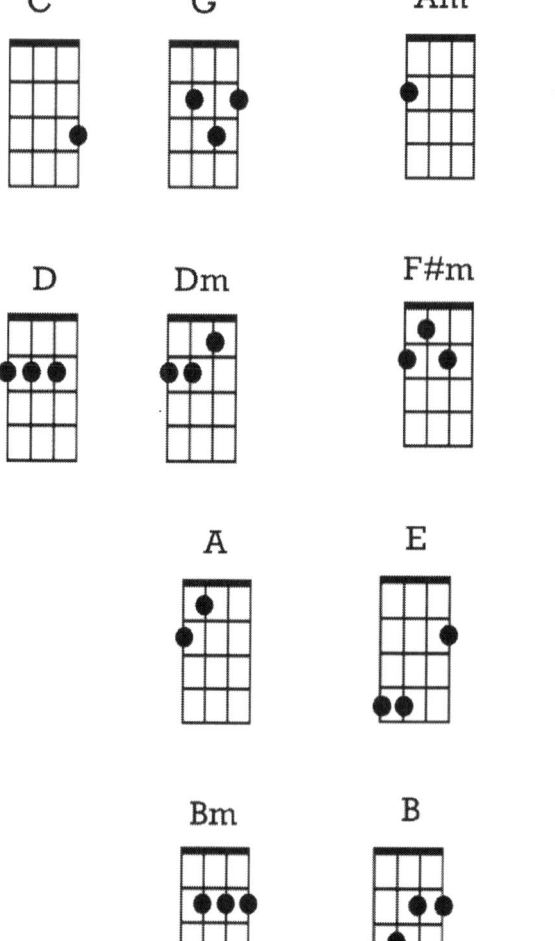

Chords

Now we're onto the topic of 'chords' - which are without a doubt, one of the most indispensable aspects of learning the ukulele. Chords are famous for being melodic and beautiful sounding - especially on the guitar but let's be frank - while they sound nice on most stringed instruments, they sound the best when played on the ukulele. There is a common belief with chords that they are simpler than melodies or finger-style ukulele but I wholeheartedly disagree. They are more or less the same in terms of level of difficulty (whatever that even means) but that's not what matters. What truly matters the most, is the application of a technique on the ukulele.

So what are **chords** and why are they so important?

In simple terms, chords are groups of two or more notes that are played (strummed) together. In essence, we take two to five notes and play them together in unison. Since chords use more than one note at a time, the misconception is that they are a hard idea to grasp. This is false. You'll actually find that once you familiarise yourself with the chord shapes, they're easier than to keep following note-for-note melodies - although both are a huge component of what it means to play the ukulele.

While this book is a songbook of 'ridiculously' easy tunes and therefore, we won't really be playing songs that involve chords played together, you **do** need to know what chords are for the sake of being a well-rounded ukulele player and secondly, there will be times in the songs where more than one note is played at the same time.

So, in order to demonstrate how a chord differs from individual notation found in tunes and melodies, we will use a **G major** chord shape.

Take a look at the diagrams at the top of the next page. Try the spot the difference.

- -

(a)

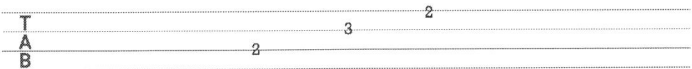

(b)

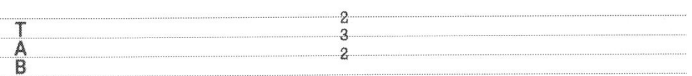

Both diagrams use the G major chord shape: that is, the second fret of the **C** string, the third fret of the **E** string and the second fret of the **A** string. The difference is clear though. Diagram (a) evidently shows single note melodies like we looked at in the previous chapter. Diagram (b) on the other hand consists of the same notes but instead of playing each note separately, you play them together. As you can see, when chords are written out on a tablature stave, they are grouped.

Basics of Metal Ukulele

In this chapter, we won't be looking at complicated theory and for all you thrashers out there, I'm afraid that we won't be teaching you how to shred on the ukulele - after all this is a beginner's songbook and it's impractical to do in the context of a ukulele book. Instead, we'll look at some very important theory which pertains to metal ukulele.

We'll be covering two things:

- **Scales**
- **Metal Riffs.**

Before we begin, there is something I quickly want to state. This songbook assumes that you know how to play and read tabs as well as chords. While this songbook is obviously for beginners, it is presumed that you've already been made aware of how ukulele players read a simplified version of sheet music called 'tablature'. Alright, now that such matters have been cleared up, we can dive on in.

Scales

We will start with looking at scales but in particular, the major scale.

But what even is a scale?

Scales are vital for understanding metal music, particularly on the ukulele. A scale is a group of music notes that are ordered in terms of pitch (from low to high) within a key. These can be major or minor. There are so many variations of scales - but in this chapter, we will be focusing on just one: the major scale - and more specifically, the 3rd mode which is called the Phrygian mode/scale.

What is a mode?

So now we must define what a mode is. Scales have 7 modes: the Ionian, Dorian, **Phrygian**, Lydian, Mixolydian, Aeolian and the Locrian. These represent how high up on the fretboard a scale is played. With the 3rd mode - metal guitarists and ukulele players often find this one to be the most useful since it is the most diverse and the most appropriate for writing metal songs. It is sometimes known as the 'secret' rock/metal element of the scales. Let's take a look at how each one is played. I will lay out each of the Phrygian scales in each key A-G for you to play and practice. We will then look at how we might apply this to a metal riff on the ukulele.

The Phrygian Scales are:

A: A Bb, C, D, E, F, G, A
B: B, C, D, Eb, G, Gb, A, B
C: C, Db, Eb, F, G, Ab, Bb, C
D: D, Eb, F, G, A, Bb, C, D
E: E, F, G, A, B, C, D, E
F: F, Gb, Ab, Bb, C, Db, Eb, F
G: G, Ab, Bb, C, D, Eb, F, G

The reason I have laid these out in this way is in case you have an accompanying musician who needs to know the notes or if you want to see the notes of the scale written out. Now, we will have a detailed look at them in tablature form so that you can practice the, in order.

A:

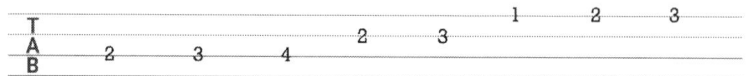

B:

C:

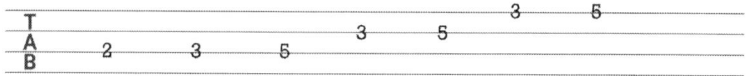

D:

E:

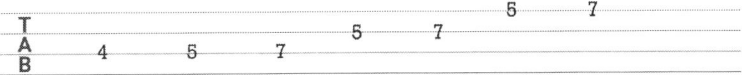

F:

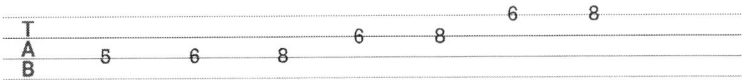

G:

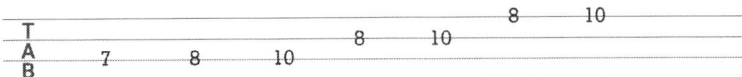

Okay then, now that we've looked at the 3rd mode of each of the major scales, it's time to apply it to metal ukulele. In order to do this, you need to choose a key to play in. It can be any note from A-G. Then, choose the Phrygian scale that matches it. The final, step is to mix up the notes of the scale in any way that sounds best to you. Since the scales contain notes which all are in one key, there are no rules.

Check out the following example in the key of E that uses the Phrygian mode of the E major scale.

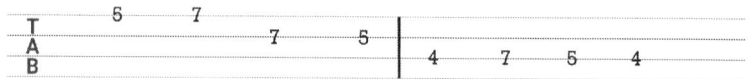

This is a simple metal riff which uses the scale with alternating orders of notes. All I did was rearrange the notes to make it sound like a riff. Try your own out below:

Riffs

The second metal technique we need to look at is riffs. These are a core component of metal ukulele.

Riffs are a series of a few notes that are the main tune to a rock song. Think of all time classics like **One** or **Sweet Child O' Mine**. They're iconic for their opening riffs. But how can such sounds be achieved on the ukulele? Simply by using our knowledge of ukulele theory and chords. I must reinstate at this stage that the second part of the book which delves into more complex metal/rock theory will help you much more to learn how to write your own riffs. Nonetheless, this chapter will introduce you to some basic riffs that you can try out.

Practice Riffs

We'll now take a look at some riffs to get us going. Each of the following riffs is in *4/4* with a 120 tempo.

Riff 1

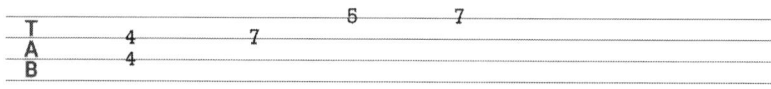

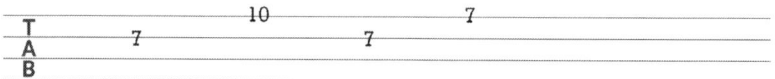

Riff 2

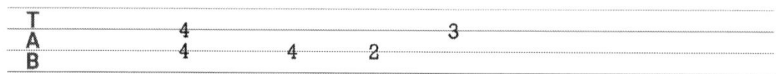

Riff 3

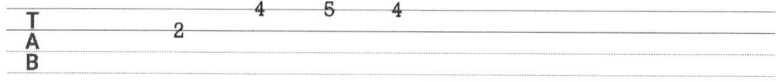

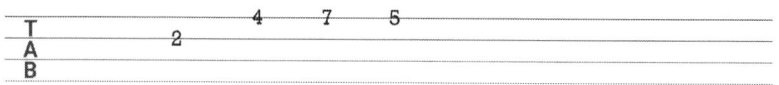

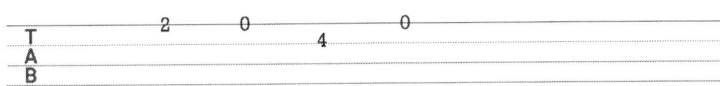

(The *2* here at the end is a whole note meaning you hold it for four counts).

Riff 4

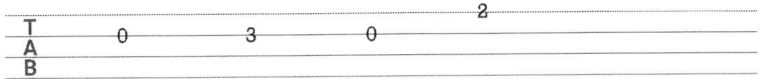

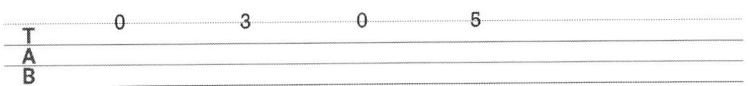

Practice the riffs slowly and build up speed with your own confidence when you feel as though you've grasped the fingerings.

Now, it's time for the songbook component. Best of luck and remember to practice each riff more than once. For reference, there is a chord chart below:

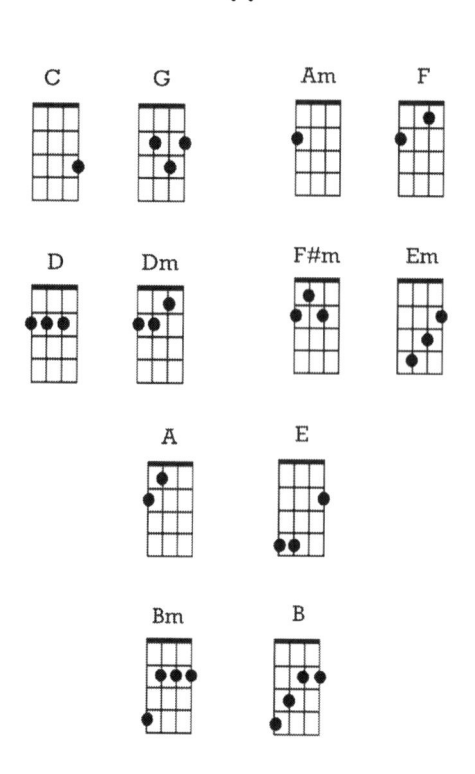

Heavy Metal Songbook

The time signature is shown alongside the 'TAB' on the left.

'Metallica' Inspired Riff:

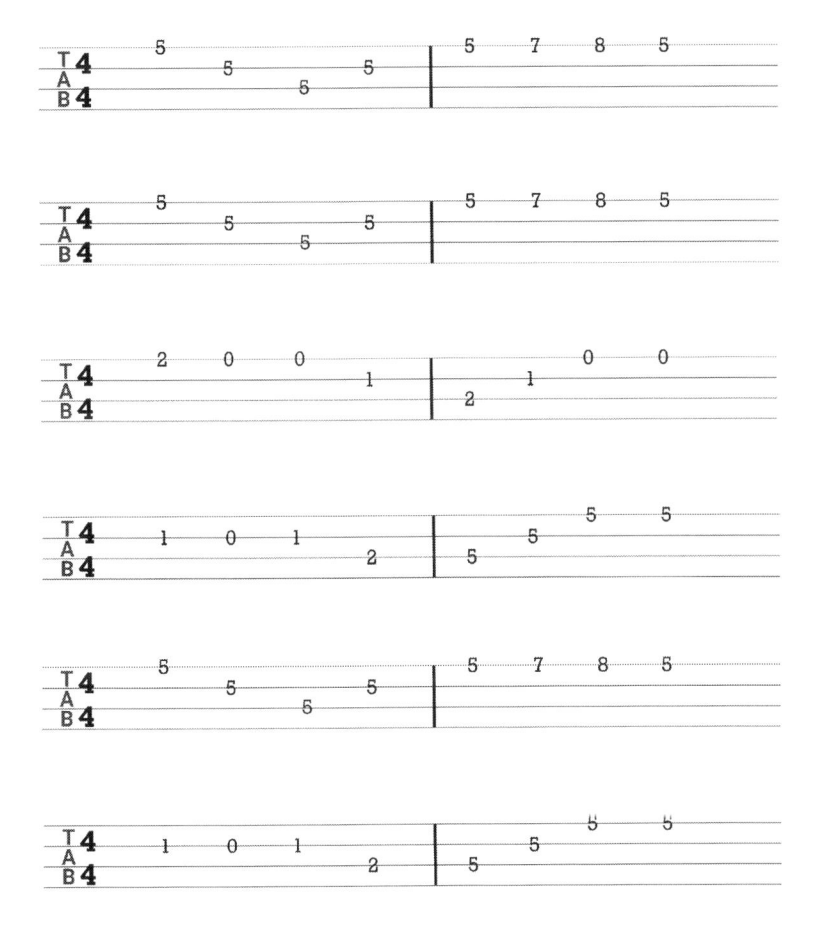

```
T 4 ---5---------------------|---5---7---8---5---
A 4-------5-------5-----------|-------------------
B 4-----------5---------------|-------------------
```

```
T 4 ---5---------------------|---5---7---8---5---
A 4-------5-------5-----------|-------------------
B 4-----------5---------------|-------------------
```

```
T 4 ---2---0---0--------------|-----------0-------0---
A 4---------------1-----------|---1-------------------
B 4---------------------------|-2---------------------
```

```
T 4 ---1---0---1--------------|-----------5-------5---
A 4---------------2-----------|---5-------------------
B 4---------------------------|-5---------------------
```

```
T 4 ---5---------------------|---5---7---8---5---
A 4-------5-------5-----------|-------------------
B 4-----------5---------------|-------------------
```

```
T 4 ---1---0---1--------------|-----------5-------5---
A 4---------------2-----------|---5-------------------
B 4---------------------------|-5---------------------
```

35

'Slipknot' Inspired Riff:

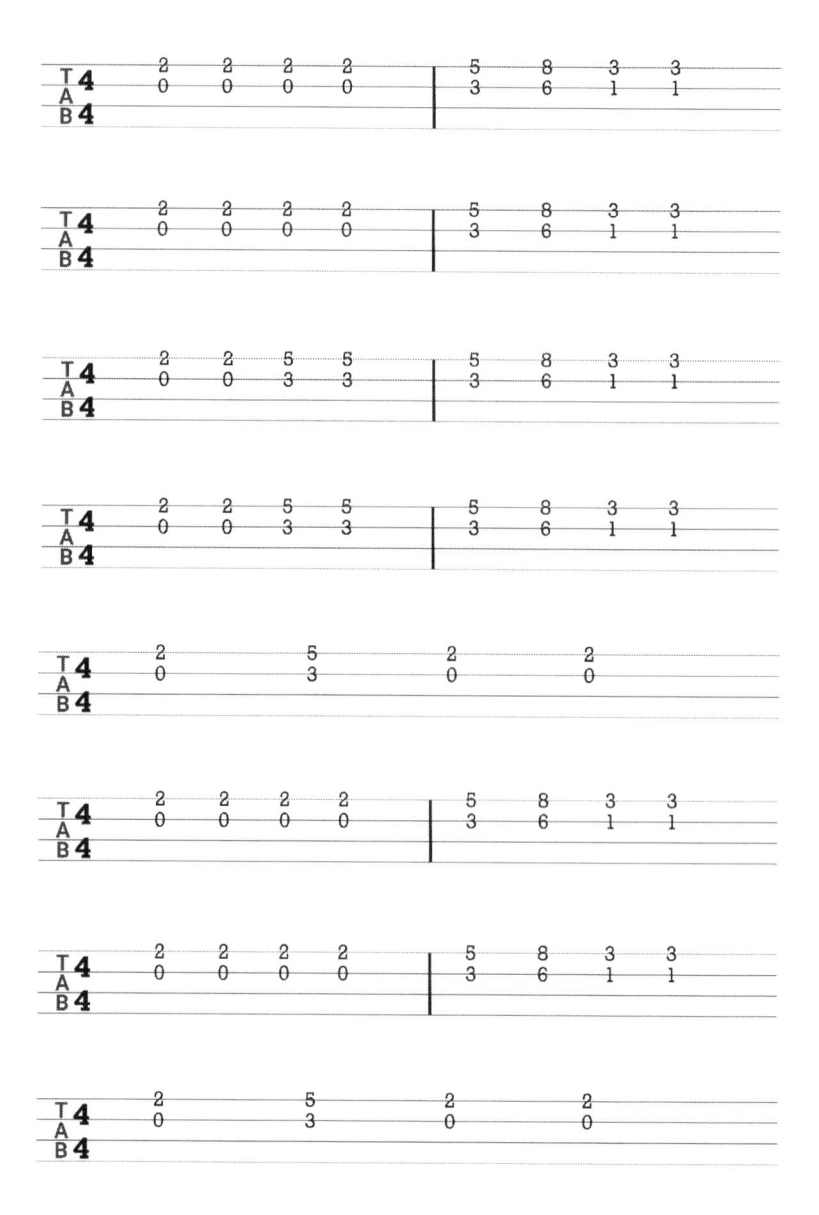

```
T|--2---2---2---2---|--5---8---3---3---|
A|--0---0---0---0---|--3---6---1---1---|
B|4-----------------|------------------|

T|--2---2---2---2---|--5---8---3---3---|
A|--0---0---0---0---|--3---6---1---1---|
B|4-----------------|------------------|

T|--2---2---5---5---|--5---8---3---3---|
A|--0---0---3---3---|--3---6---1---1---|
B|4-----------------|------------------|

T|--2---2---5---5---|--5---8---3---3---|
A|--0---0---3---3---|--3---6---1---1---|
B|4-----------------|------------------|

T|--2-------5-------2-------2-------|
A|--0-------3-------0-------0-------|
B|4---------------------------------|

T|--2---2---2---2---|--5---8---3---3---|
A|--0---0---0---0---|--3---6---1---1---|
B|4-----------------|------------------|

T|--2---2---2---2---|--5---8---3---3---|
A|--0---0---0---0---|--3---6---1---1---|
B|4-----------------|------------------|

T|--2-------5-------2-------2-------|
A|--0-------3-------0-------0-------|
B|4---------------------------------|
```

'Bullet For My Valentine' Inspired Riff:

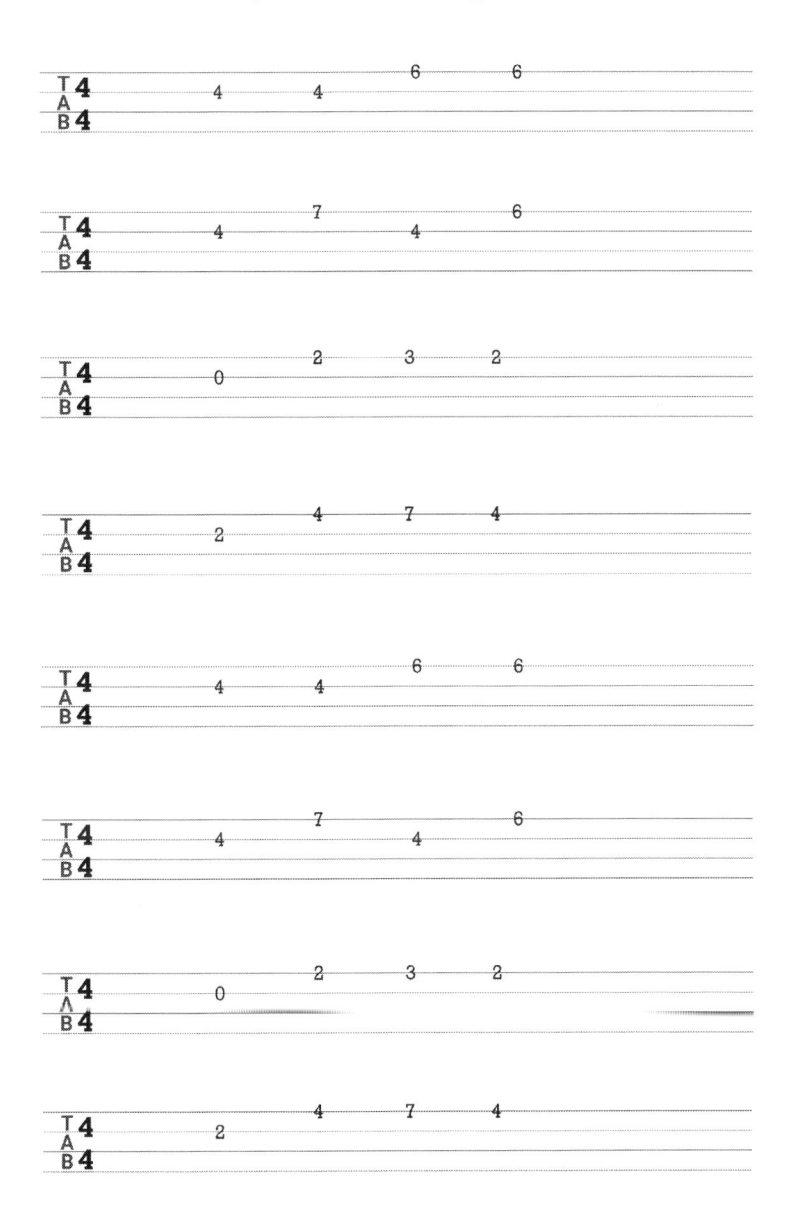

```
T|4--------4---------4---------6---------6---------|
A|4-----------------------------------------------|
B|4-----------------------------------------------|

T|4--------4---------7---------4---------6---------|
A|4-----------------------------------------------|
B|4-----------------------------------------------|

T|4--------0---------2---------3---------2---------|
A|4-----------------------------------------------|
B|4-----------------------------------------------|

T|4--------2---------4---------7---------4---------|
A|4-----------------------------------------------|
B|4-----------------------------------------------|

T|4--------4---------4---------6---------6---------|
A|4-----------------------------------------------|
B|4-----------------------------------------------|

T|4--------4---------7---------4---------6---------|
A|4-----------------------------------------------|
B|4-----------------------------------------------|

T|4--------0---------2---------3---------2---------|
A|4-----------------------------------------------|
B|4-----------------------------------------------|

T|4--------2---------4---------7---------4---------|
A|4-----------------------------------------------|
B|4-----------------------------------------------|
```

'M. Manson' Inspired Riff:

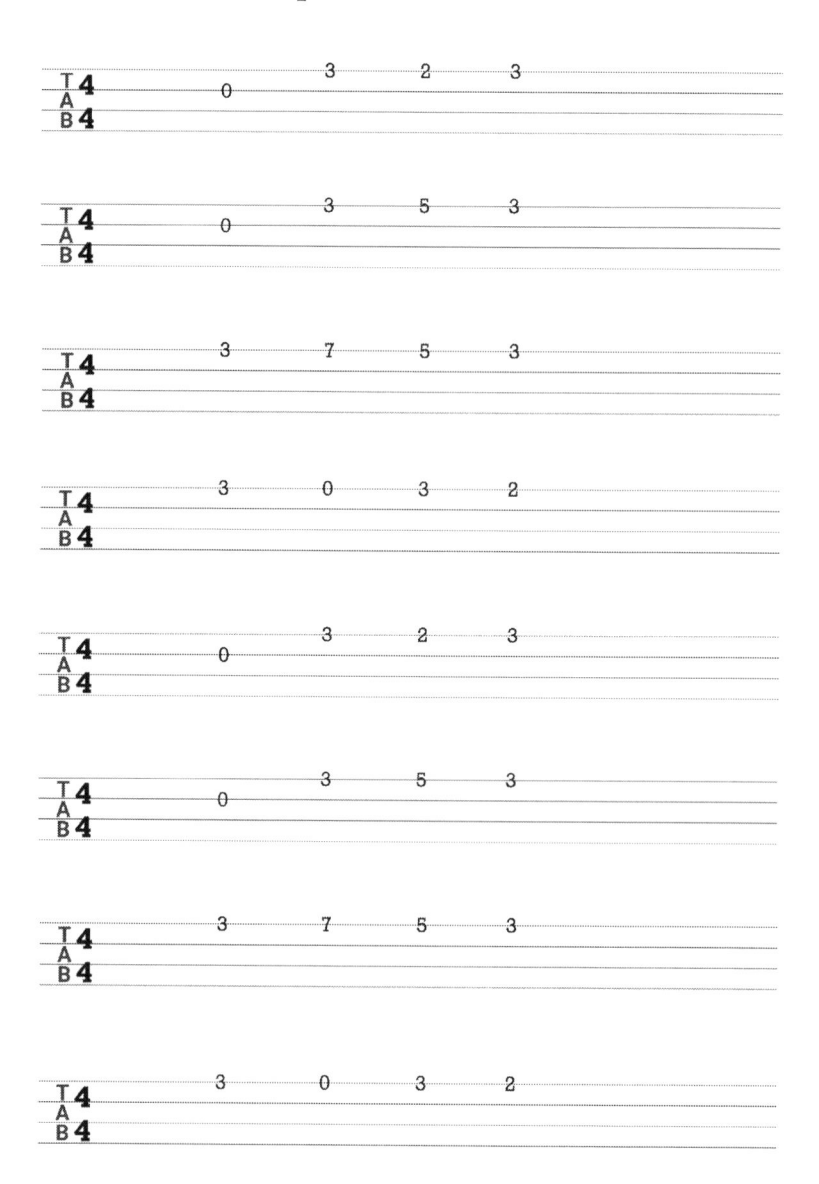

```
T|4---0---3---2---3-------|
A|4-----------------------|
B|4-----------------------|

T|4---0---3---5---3-------|
A|4-----------------------|
B|4-----------------------|

T|4---3---7---5---3-------|
A|4-----------------------|
B|4-----------------------|

T|4---3---0---3---2-------|
A|4-----------------------|
B|4-----------------------|

T|4---0---3---2---3-------|
A|4-----------------------|
B|4-----------------------|

T|4---0---3---5---3-------|
A|4-----------------------|
B|4-----------------------|

T|4---3---7---5---3-------|
A|4-----------------------|
B|4-----------------------|

T|4---3---0---3---2-------|
A|4-----------------------|
B|4-----------------------|
```

'Saosin' Inspired Riff:

```
T|4--------5-----8----7----5--------|
A|4--------------------------------|
B|4--------------------------------|

T|4--------6-----8----7----10-------|
A|4--------------------------------|
B|4--------------------------------|

T|4--------5-----8----7----5--------|
A|4--------------------------------|
B|4--------------------------------|

T|4-----------3----2----3----2------|
A|4--------------------------------|
B|4--------------------------------|

T|4--------5-----8----7----5--------|
A|4--------------------------------|
B|4--------------------------------|

T|4--------6-----8----7----10-------|
A|4--------------------------------|
B|4--------------------------------|

T|4--------5-----8----7----5--------|
A|4--------------------------------|
B|4--------------------------------|

T|4-----------3----2----3----2------|
A|4--------------------------------|
B|4--------------------------------|

T|4------------------0--------------|
A|4--------------------------------|
B|4--------------------------------|
```

'Lamb of God' Inspired Riff:

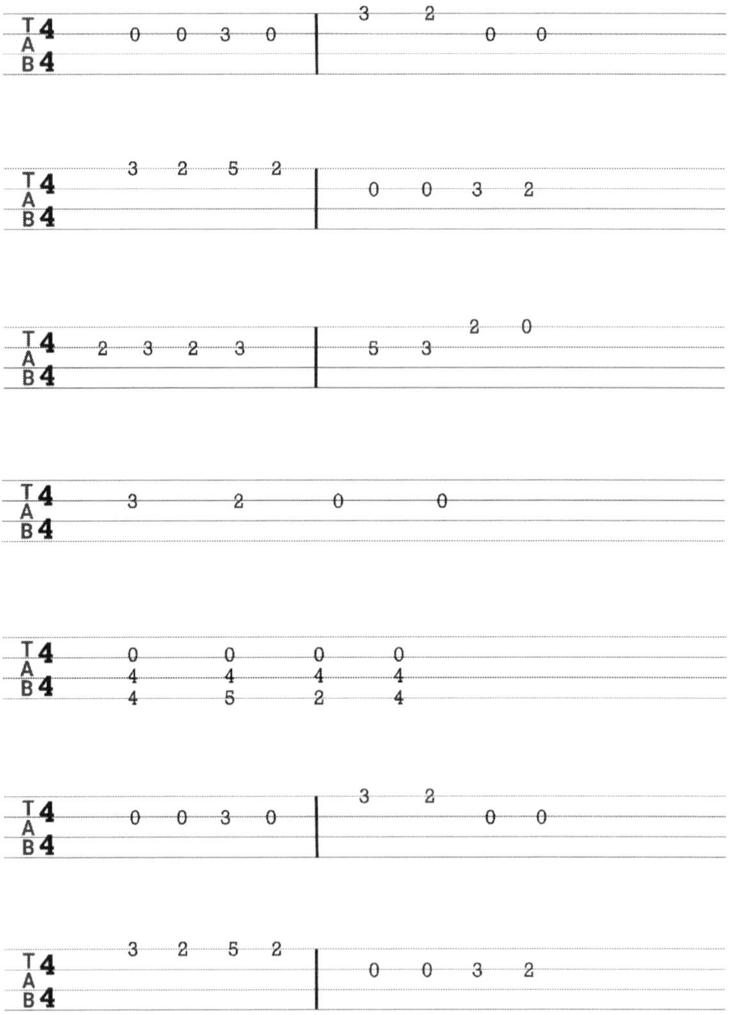

```
T|4---0--0--3--0----|---3---2--------0--0----|
A|4-----------------|------------------------|
B|4-----------------|------------------------|

T|4---3--2--5--2----|---0--0--3--2-----------|
A|4-----------------|------------------------|
B|4-----------------|------------------------|

T|4---------------------|-----------2--0-----|
A|4---2--3--2--3--------|---5--3-------------|
B|4---------------------|--------------------|

T|4---3----2----0----0----|
A|4-----------------------|
B|4-----------------------|

T|4---0----0----0----0----|
A|4---4----4----4----4----|
B|4---4----5----2----4----|

T|4---0--0--3--0----|---3---2--------0--0----|
A|4-----------------|------------------------|
B|4-----------------|------------------------|

T|4---3--2--5--2----|---0--0--3--2-----------|
A|4-----------------|------------------------|
B|4-----------------|------------------------|
```

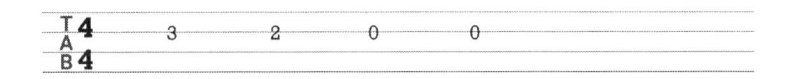

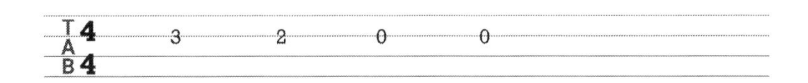

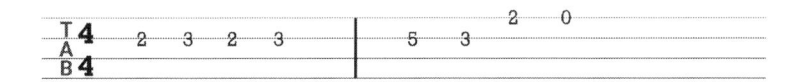

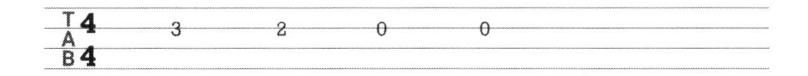

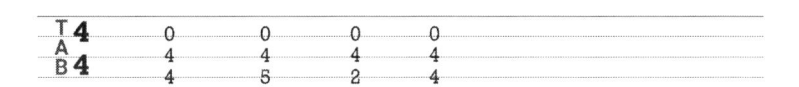

```
T|4--2--3--2--3----|----5--3--2--0----
A|4----------------|------------------
B|4----------------|------------------

T|4----3----2----0----0----
A|4------------------------
B|4------------------------

T|4----3----2----0----0----
A|4------------------------
B|4------------------------

T|4--2--3--2--3----|----5--3--2--0----
A|4----------------|------------------
B|4----------------|------------------

T|4----3----2----0----0----
A|4------------------------
B|4------------------------

T|4--0----0----0----0--
A|4--4----4----4----4--
B|4--4----5----2----4--
```

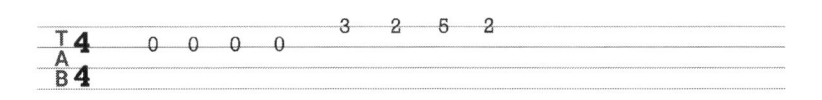

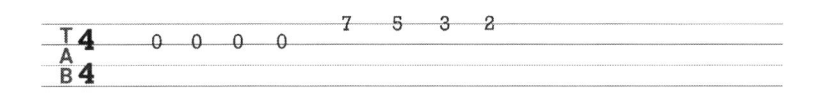

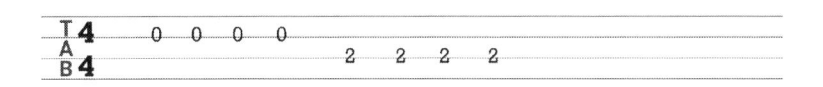

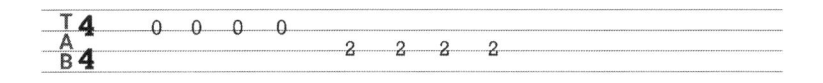

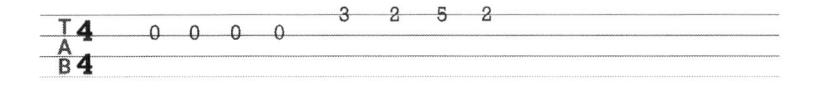

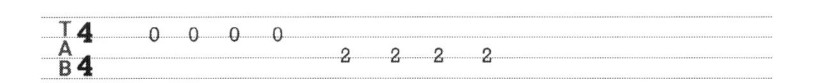

'CANDY' Inspired Riff:

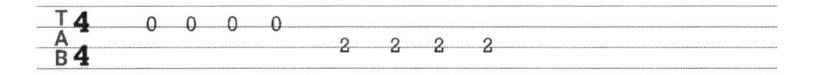

```
T|4--0--0--0--0--3--2--5--2--|
A|4-------------------------|
B|4-------------------------|

T|4--0--0--0--0--7--5--3--2--|
A|4-------------------------|
B|4-------------------------|

T|4--0--0--0--0-------------|
A|4-------------2--2--2--2--|
B|4-------------------------|

T|4--0--0--0--0-------------|
A|4-------------2--2--2--2--|
B|4-------------------------|

T|4--0--0--0--0--3--2--5--2--|
A|4-------------------------|
B|4-------------------------|

T|4--0--0--0--0-------------|
A|4-------------------------|
B|4-------------2--2--2--2--|

T|4--0--0--0--0-------------|
A|4-------------------------|
B|4-------------2--2--2--2--|
```

```
T|--0--0--0--0--3--2--5--2----|
A|----------------------------|
B|----------------------------|
```

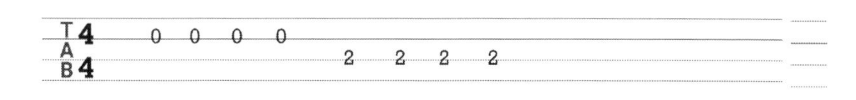

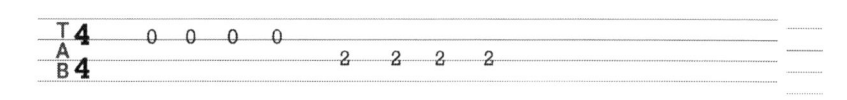

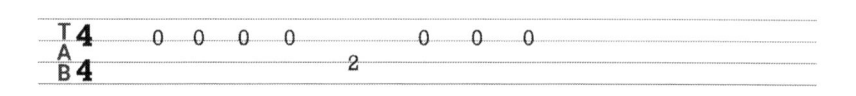

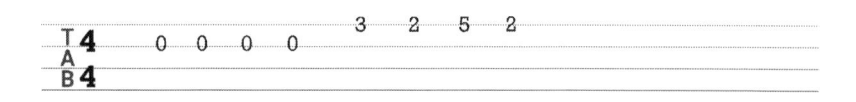

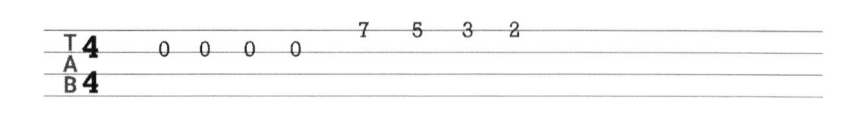

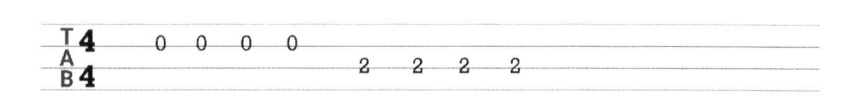

```
T|--0--0--0--0----------------|
A|--------------2--2--2--2----|
B|----------------------------|
```

```
T|--0--0--0--0----------------|
A|--------------2--2--2--2----|
B|----------------------------|
```

```
T|--0--0--0--0-----0--0--0----|
A|--------------2-------------|
B|----------------------------|
```

```
T|--0--0--0--0--3--2--5--2----|
A|----------------------------|
B|----------------------------|
```

```
T|--0--0--0--0--7--5--3--2----|
A|----------------------------|
B|----------------------------|
```

```
T|--0--0--0--0----------------|
A|--------------2--2--2--2----|
B|----------------------------|
```

'Black Sabbath' Inspired Riff:

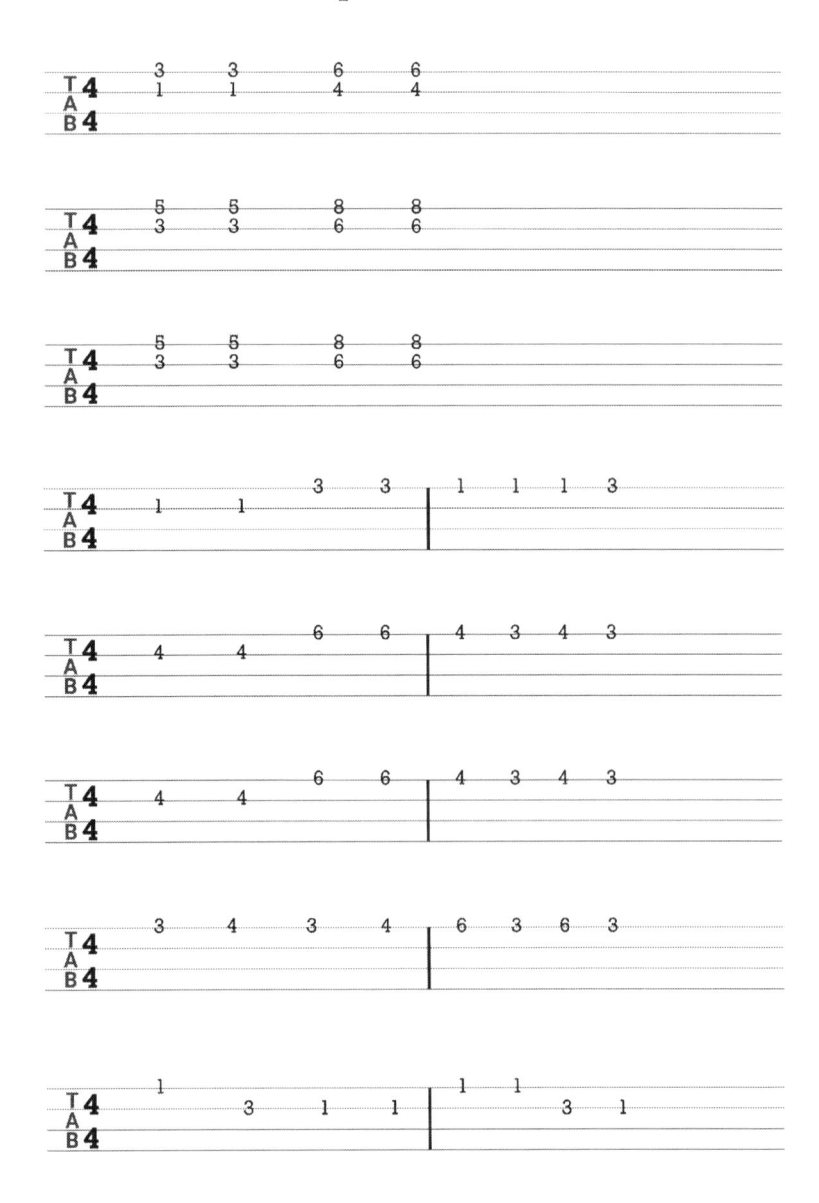

```
T|--3---3------6---6----------------------|
A|--1---1------4---4----------------------|
B|----------------------------------------|

T|--5---5------8---8----------------------|
A|--3---3------6---6----------------------|
B|----------------------------------------|

T|--5---5------8---8----------------------|
A|--3---3------6---6----------------------|
B|----------------------------------------|

T|--1---1------3---3---|--1--1--1--3------|
A|---------------------|------------------|
B|---------------------|------------------|

T|-------------6---6---|--4--3--4--3------|
A|--4---4--------------|------------------|
B|---------------------|------------------|

T|-------------6---6---|--4--3--4--3------|
A|--4---4--------------|------------------|
B|---------------------|------------------|

T|--3--4--3--4---------|--6--3--6--3------|
A|---------------------|------------------|
B|---------------------|------------------|

T|--1-------1--1-------|--1--1------------|
A|-----3--------1------|--------3----1----|
B|---------------------|------------------|
```

```
T|4--3---3---6---6--------
A|4--1---1---4---4--------
B|4----------------------
```

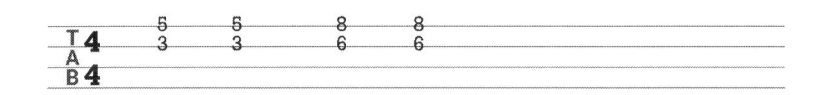

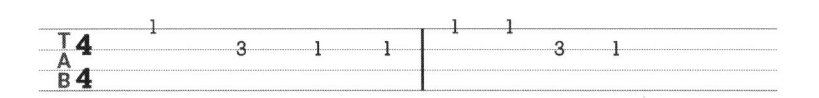

```
T|4--5---5---8---8--------
A|4--3---3---6---6--------
B|4----------------------
```

```
T|4--1------------|--1---1------
A|4-----3---1---1-|------3---1--
B|4---------------|------------
```

'Cradle Of Filth' Inspired Riff:

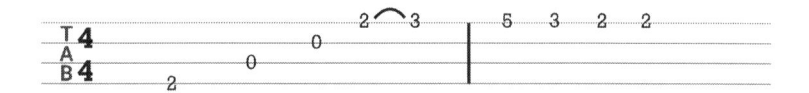

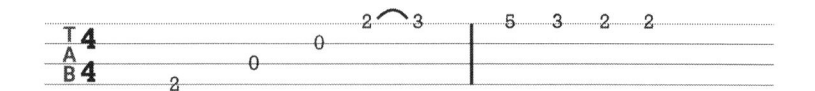

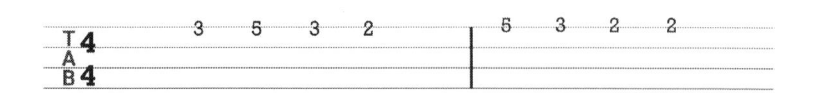

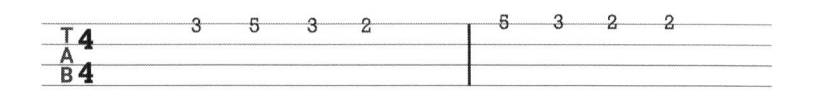

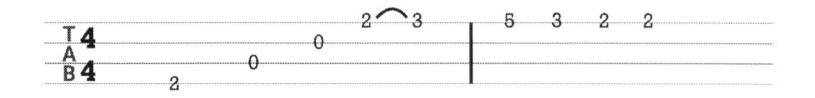

Schizoid

(Verse)

    Am
I got a pain in my chest (woah!)

    Am
I got a pain in my chest (woah!)

    Am   F
I got a pain in my head like a f*cking train

    Am   F
just smashed into my f*cking brain

  G
and I'm not the one who's getting out

F
I'm not the man who will save you like some hero

clown

Am   F

at the back of the bar in the pouring rain

Am   F

my head is filled with thoughts that'd make you think I was insane

(Chorus)

C   F   Am   G

And that's me!

C   F   Am   G

That's just me!

C

Schizoid, me!

(Verse)

Am

I got a pain in my mind (woah!)

Am

Never turn around to look behind (woah!)

Am   F

I got a pain in my throat like I swallowed coal

Am   F

With every year that I swallow more and more

G

and I'm not the one who's getting out

F

of society providing more and more doubt

Am   F

at the back of the street in the soldering sun

Am   F

my head is filled with thought that'd make me want to give up

(Chorus)

C F Am G

And that's me!

C F Am G

That's just me!

C

Schizoid, me!

(Chorus)

C   F   Am   G

And that's me!

C   F   Am   G

That's just me!

C

Schizoid, me!

Afterlife

(Intro)

Em   C   D   Em

(Verse)

Em
I wanted more than they could ever give me

C
Stuck in a world where there's nothing but hatred

Em
I would slit my own throat to be free

C
Of all of this….

Em
Preoccupied with a sense of dread

C

Letting these fears run through my head

Em

I'm eating my shame down to the core

C

Digging myself an even bigger hole

(Chorus)

G

I took the news like a sharp knife

C

I couldn't even look you in the eyes

Em

Sent me on the wave of a downward spiral

D   Em

In an afterlife of crazy fantasy

Em C D Em

(Verse)

Em

I wanted more than you ever gave me

C

Stuck in your mind where there's nothing but violence

Em

I would slit my own throat to be free

C

Of all of you….

Em

Preoccupied with a sense of dread

C

Letting these fears run through my head

Em

I'm eating your shame down to the core

C

You couldn't dig yourself a bigger hole,

D

even if you tried!

(Chorus)

G

I took the news like a sharp knife

C

I couldn't even look you in the eyes

Em

Sent me on the wave of a downward spiral

D　　　　　　　Em

In an afterlife of crazy fantasy

G

I took the news like a sharp knife

C

I couldn't even look you in the eyes

Em

Sent me on the wave of a downward spiral

D　　　　　　　Em

In an afterlife of crazy fantasy.

. .

End song on 'Em'.

Casket

(Intro)

Bm   G   F#m

Bm   G   F#m

Verse

Bm

Fading into the abyss

G

Crumbling under the emptiness

Bm   G   Bm

It seems so dumb, 'you're only numb'

Bm

I tell myself through all of this

Bm   G   Bm

The power in the house is out

Bm

What difference could it make?

G   A

I know what this life's all about.

Chorus

D

Saving my pain for a better cause

A

Wasting away from the hand of cards

Bm   F#m G F#m   Bm

I've been dealt! *(screamed)*

Bm	F#m G F#m	Bm

I've been dealt! (*screamed*)

Bm	G	F#m

Bm	G	F#m

(Verse)

Bm

Soon I'll have a casket on my own

G

I'll slip right in, my eternal home

Bm	G	Bm

It seems so dumb, 'you're only numb'

Bm

I tell myself through all of this

Bm	G	Bm

The love inside has worn me thin

Bm

Emotionless, boned and stripped

G	A

I know what this life's all about.

Chorus

D

Saving my pain for a better cause

A

Wasting away from the hand of cards

Bm	F#m	G	F#m	Bm

I've been dealt! *(screamed)*

| Bm | F#m | G | F#m | Bm |

I've been dealt! (screamed)

'Linkin Park' Inspired Riff:

```
T|4-------2-------4-------4-------2-------|
A|4---------------------------------------|
B|4---------------------------------------|

T|4-------0-------0-------0-------4-------|
A|4---------------------------------------|
B|4---------------------------------------|

T|4-------2-------4-------4-------2-------|
A|4---------------------------------------|
B|4---------------------------------------|

T|4-------0-------0-------0-------4-------|
A|4---------------------------------------|
B|4---------------------------------------|

T|4-------2-------0-------2-------0-------|
A|4---------------------------------------|
B|4---------------------------------------|

T|4-------2-------0-------4-------0-------|
A|4---------------------------------------|
B|4---------------------------------------|

T|4-------2-------4-------4-------2-------|
A|4---------------------------------------|
B|4---------------------------------------|
```

```
T|4----------0-------0-------0---------------|
A|-----------------------------------4-------|
B|4------------------------------------------|


T|4----------2-------0-------4---------------|
A|-------------------------------------------|
B|4------------------------------------------|
```

'Stone Sour' Inspired Riff:

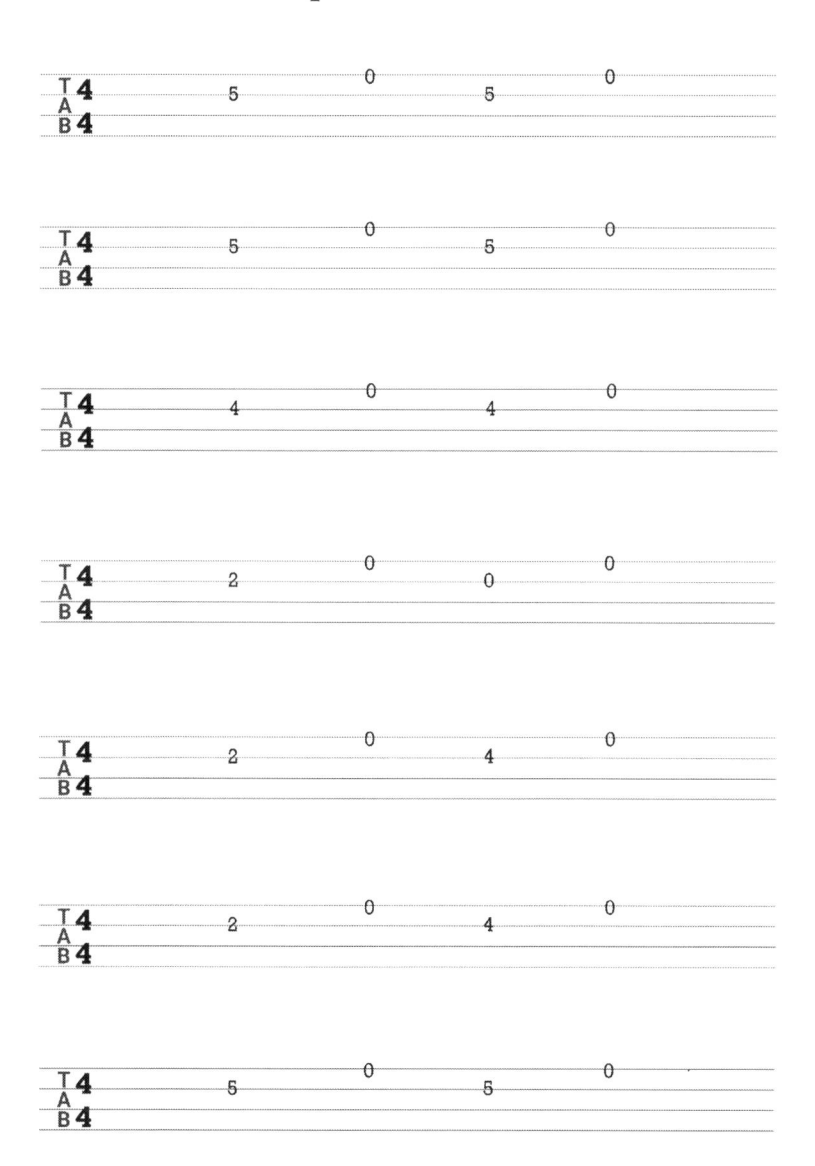

```
T|--------------0-----------------0-------|
A|----5---------------5-------------------|
B|----------------------------------------|

T|--------------0-----------------0-------|
A|----5---------------5-------------------|
B|----------------------------------------|

T|--------------0-----------------0-------|
A|----4---------------4-------------------|
B|----------------------------------------|

T|--------------0-----------------0-------|
A|----2---------------0-------------------|
B|----------------------------------------|

T|--------------0-----------------0-------|
A|----2---------------4-------------------|
B|----------------------------------------|

T|--------------0-----------------0-------|
A|----2---------------4-------------------|
B|----------------------------------------|

T|--------------0-----------------0-------|
A|----5---------------5-------------------|
B|----------------------------------------|
```

```
T|4-----------------4--------0-----------4--------0-----------|
A|4-----------------------------------------------------------|
B|4-----------------------------------------------------------|


T|4-----------------2--------0-----------0--------0-----------|
A|4-----------------------------------------------------------|
B|4-----------------------------------------------------------|


T|4-----------------2--------0-----------4--------0-----------|
A|4-----------------------------------------------------------|
B|4-----------------------------------------------------------|


T|4--------------------------5--------------------------------|
A|4-----------------------------------------------------------|
B|4-----------------------------------------------------------|
```

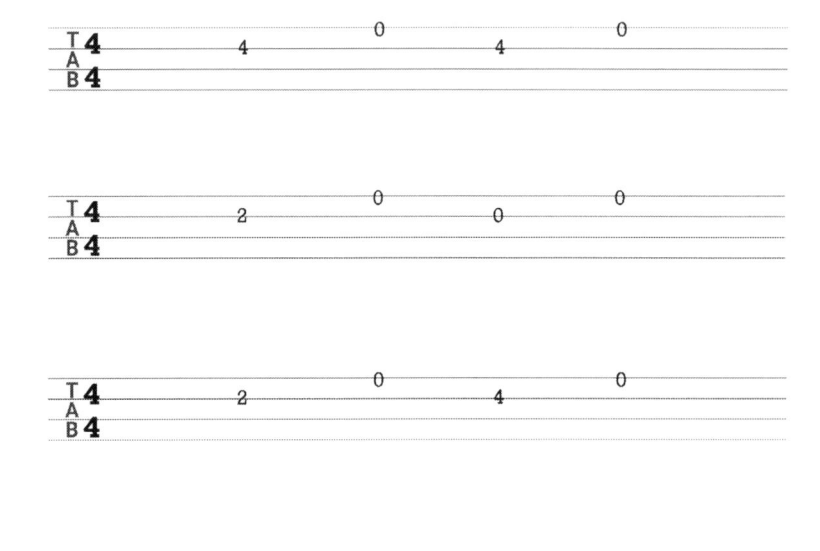

Conclusion

We come to the end of this metal hits songbook ! I hope you enjoyed all the riffs and tunes on offer and I would like to thank you one last time for choosing this book! All the best!

COPYRIGHT

A&M BOOKS

2018

Printed in Great Britain
by Amazon